# Economics:

## Foundation of Economics

HEMANTA SAIKIA

**ISBN: 1516988345**
**ISBN-13:** 978-1516988341

# DEDICATION

To my parents and other family members.

# CONTENTS

# ACKNOWLEDGMENTS

I would also like to give my special thanks to my family whose patient love enabled me to complete this work. I extend due respect and gratitude to all those who helps and co-operations will be valuable and precious for all time to come before me.

# 1 AN INTRODUCTION

As a social science, Economics describes what is happening in the economic system rather it attempts to explain how it maneuvers and make predictions about what may happen to economic variables

Economics made progress without mathematics, but has made faster progress with it. Mathematics has brought transparency to many hundreds of economic arguments. - Deirdre N. Mccloskey (1994)

in future; for example, it predicts the potential speculation, profits, saving, prices of goods and services etc. In this regard, mathematics is fundamental to any grave application of economics to these areas. The quantification of economic variables is another important aspect of the economic analysis. In the process of simple demand analysis, we often predict the behavior of the demand in terms of commodity price. Economics needs to determine how much demand is predictable to change if price is changed by a explicit amount. Thus quantification of economics requires the use of mathematics. This book amalgamated both theoretical parts and tools, so that students without having theoretical knowledge on economics can learn application of tools in Economics. We hope that students of both Economics and other disciplines especially the management students can learn economics from the point of view of practical life.

In modern times, the whole economic system of analysis is seemed to be integrated with mathematics and statistics and quantitative economics is now an integral part of economics. However it is not a distinct branch of economic rather it is an approach to the economics in which it uses mathematical symbols for the statement of the economic theories and for reasoning. In this part of the book, we will discuss the meaning of Economics and application of Mathematics in economics, its nature and the relationship with other branches of economics.

## 2 WHAT IS ECONOMICS?

The social sciences look for the activities of the people and their social activities. What makes economics poles apart from the other social sciences is the models economists exercise. If a general person ask you a question: What is Economics? You need to simplify your answer and you may say that Economics is the study of how people decide to assign their scarce resources. We must go back to the basic human requirements i.e. food, cloth and shelter. Till the Industrial Revolution, the enormous preponderance of the world's population thrashed about for right of entry to basic human needs. For fulfilling these basic needs of human life, we need money. Now, the question may again arise: why we require money? Money is required to purchase them. Since these things are limited, so there is a value and so money which act as a

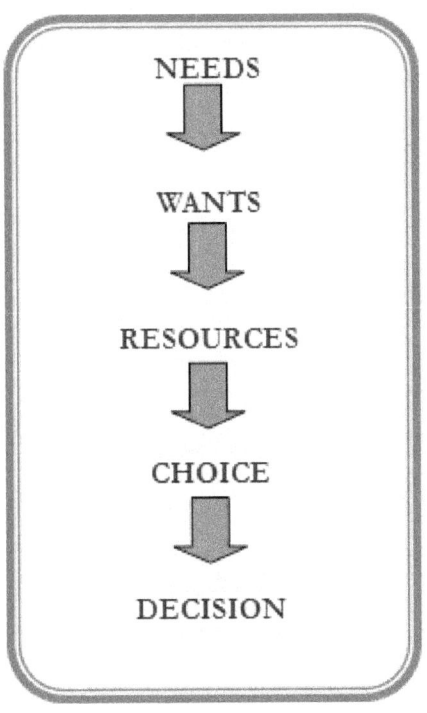

intermediate of exchange, required to purchase them. But, keep remember that human beings have limitless wants. You need money to purchase book, bicycle, to travel etc. But the money that you can acquire through stiff working or through labour works is limited and so you can't spent it for satisfying all of your wants. Whilst the fundamental needs of survival are imperative in the function of the economy, wants are the prevailing force which stimulates requirement for goods and services. So, what you will do? You will choose the important wants and spend the money on it or allocate it a desire way. To facilitate the economic resources, economists must categorize the nature and diverse wants of consumers, in addition to prioritize wants and organize production to satisfy as many wants as possible. These wants are often termed into *individual wants*, which relly on the individual's preferences and purchasing power and *collective wants*, those of total groups of people. Generally, Economic models assume people are rational (with well-ordered preferences), want to maximize something (such as profits or satisfaction), and then do the best they can give their scarce resources. Food and clothing can be classified as either needs or desires, stepping on what type and how often a good is asked for. Wants are effective desires for a particular product, or something which can only be obtained by working for it. Now, you can term Economic a medium of analysis for allocating scarce resources linking money with wants and as a means to fulfill them.

**?** What do you mean by resources?

Δ Resources are those elements that a nation has at its disposal to deal with the issue of scarcity. Resources are the inputs used in the production of things which we need. The resources which include (i) natural resources (land, mineral, forest etc.) (ii) Human resources (iii) manmade resources (machinery, building etc.) and (iv) enterprise are scarce. They are not found in as much quantity as we need them.

The economic problem essentially rotates around the thought of choice, which ultimately must answer the problem. Because of the inadequate resources accessible, producers must decide what to generate first to please requirements. Here, consumers are considered the chief power of the choice and the goods which they desire must also vigorous within their funds and purchasing power parity. A household or country has to manage resources of the country or you can say public avenues for which it has to deals with decisions of scarcity and choice. Scarcity implies that limited resources and therefore cannot accomplish all of the needs by producing all the goods or services people wish to have. Just as your father cannot give everything he or she wants, a society cannot give every individual the highest standard of living to which he or she might aspire. Economics is the study of how society manages its scarce resources. In most societies, resources are allocated not by, planners, millions of households and firms. Economics therefore examine how to make economic decisions: how much they produce, what they produce, how they produce, and whom they allocate these goods. Economics also study how economic agents interact with one another. For instance, they examine how the buyers and sellers of a good together determine the price at which the good is sold and the quantity that is sold. Finally, economics analyze nature and trends of economy in total, including the growth in average income, etc.

## ECONOMICS: ACCORDING TO ECONOMISTS

The term *economics* comes from the Ancient Greek 'οἰκονομία'. The English term *'oikonomia'* implies management of a household, administration hence 'rules of the household'. Management of household implies wants-income-choice-decision. So, it studies rules of managing a household. In fact, the same is true for a society also.

If we consider the whole society as a people, then the societies also faces the dilemma of tackling unlimited wants of the members of the activities, and have arrived at different definitions of Economics.

We shall now discuss some of these definitions in detail. These definitions can be classified into four groups:

(a) Wealth definition

(b) Material welfare definition

(c) Scarcity definition and

(d) Growth Centered definition.

## 1. Wealth Definitions of Economics

In the evolution of Economics, first we can take the name of **Adam Smith,** a Scottish philosopher who was later known as the *'Father of Economics'*. Adam Smith (1776) defined what was then called 'political economy' as *"An inquiry into the nature and causes of the wealth of nations"*, in meticulous as:

> *"A branch of the science of a statesman or legislator [with the twofold objectives of providing] a plentiful revenue or subsistence for the people ... [and] to supply the state or commonwealth with a revenue for the public services"* J. B. Say, a French classical economist, described economics as the science which treats of wealth" J. S. Mill another classical economist in the middle of 19th century looked upon economics "as the practical science of production and distribution of wealth'. According to Malthus "Man is motivated by self interest only The desire to collect wealth never leaves him till he goes into the grave". The main points of the definitions of economics given by the above classical economists are that (1) economics is the study of wealth only. It deals with consumption, production, exchange and distribution aspects of wealth." (2) Only those material goods which are scarce are included in wealth.

According to Adam Smith, Economics, is a branch of the science of a statesman or lawmaker, recommends two distinct objects: (1) to supply a abundant returns or survival for the people, or more properly to facilitate them to provide such a income or subsistence for themselves; (2) to provide the state with income adequate for the community services. It proposes to augment both the citizens and the sovereign.

Adam Smith

Adam Smith (5 June 1723 OS – 17 July 1790) was a Scottish moral philosopher and a pioneer of political economy. One of the key figures of the Scottish Enlightenment, Adam Smith is best known for two classic works: *The Theory of Moral Sentiments* (1759), and **An Inquiry into the Nature and Causes of the Wealth of Nations** (1776).

Earlier, Economics was termed as political economy. **'Political'** derives from the Greek term (polos) for the city-state, the fundamental unit of political organization in the classical period. Political economy therefore originated in the management of the family and political households. Writing fifteen years before Smith's Wealth of Nations, Steuart (1967: 2) made the connection by noting that "*What economy is in a family, political economy is in a state.*" Thus, the term political economy means the administration of the assets of the state.

Adam Smith, the father of modem Economics, in his book entitled **'An Enquiry into the Nature and Causes of the Wealth of Nations' (Published in 1776)** defined Economics *"as a study of wealth. Smith considered the acquisition of wealth as the main objective of human activity"*. According to him the theme matter of Economics is the lessons of how wealth is shaped and devoted. As a result, Smith's definition is known as wealth definition in Economics. He presumed that, the better-off a nation becomes the better-off are its citizens. Thus, it is imperative to find out, how a country can be wealthy. Economics is the subject matter that tells us how to make a nation well-heeled. The definition of Economics, as science of wealth, had some points.

What is Wealth?

Wealth in Adam Smith definition of Economics implies those material goods that are efficient for use and scarce.

**1. Emphasis on wealth:** These wealth centered definitions gave too much importance to the creation of wealth in an economy. The classical economists like Adam Smith, Richardo, J.B. Say and others believed that economic affluence of any nation depends only on the growth of wealth. It highlighted an important problem faced by each and every nation of the world, namely formation of wealth.

**2. Inquiry into the formation of wealth:** These definitions illustrate that Economics also deals with an investigation into the causes at the back of the formation of wealth. For instance, prosperity of a nation may be augmented through raising the altitude of production and sell abroad. Since, the problems of scarcity, redundancy etc. can be solved to a greater extent when wealth is produced and is disseminated justifiably; it goes to the credit of Adam Smith and his followers to have addressed to the problems of economic growth and increase in the production of wealth.

**3. A study on the nature of wealth:** These descriptions have specified that prosperity of a nation includes only material goods and non-material commodities are not incorporated. Hence, non-material goods like services of educators, doctors, etc., are not considered as 'wealth'.

The study of Economics as a **'Science of Wealth'** has been criticized on several grounds. However, the definitions given by Adam Smith and other classical economists were severely disparaged by social scientists. They named economics as a *'dismal science'* and a *"science of getting rich"*. Ruskin dubbed Admn Smith as the *"half bred and half witted man"*. The main criticisms levied on these definitions are as under:

**(1) Too much weightage on wealth:**

The definitions of economics given by classical economists provide chief importance to wealth and lesser importance to man. The fact is that the learning of man is more important than the study of wealth.

(2) **Narrow meaning of wealth:**

The word **'wealth'** in the classical economists definitions of economics means only material goods such as chair, book, pen, etc.

These do not include non-material goods such as services of doctors, nurses, soldiers etc.

### (3) Notion of economic man:

According to wealth definitions, man works only for his self-interest and social interest is demoted in the background. Marshall and his supporters were of the view that economics does not study a self-interested man but a general man.

### (3) No talk about Human being's welfare.

The "Wealth" definitions disregard the importance of human being's welfare. Prosperity is not the be all and the end all of all human activities.

### (4) It does not study means:

The definitions of economics lay weightage on the earning of wealth as an end in itself. They disregard the means or resources which are limited for the earning of wealth.

**(6)** The explanation of economics given by classical economists were excessively criticized by the literary writers of that time. The central argument of the book 'Wealth of Nations" was that the market economy allowed every individual to add his maximum to the production of wealth of nation still not only holds good but is also being experienced and supported throughout the capitalistic world. Since the word 'wealth' did not have a apparent connotation, therefore the description of economics became contentious. It was regarded as irrational and narrow. Latterly of 19th century, Alfred Marshall gave his own definition of economics and therein he laid stress on man and his welfare.

## Who were classical economists?

Classical economics is widely regarded as the first modern school of economic thought. Its major developers include Adam Smith, Jean-Baptiste Say, David Ricardo, Thomas Malthus and John Stuart Mill. Adam Smith's *The Wealth of Nations* in 1776 is usually considered to mark the beginning of classical economics.

## MATERIAL WELFARE DEFINITIONS OF ECONOMICS

Alfred Marshall in 1890 in his book *'Principle of Political Economy'* also stressed out the importance of wealth. But he also emphasized the function of the individual in the formation and the use of wealth.

> According to Marshall, 'Economics is a study of mankind in the ordinary business of life, how he gets his income and how he spends it. Thus it is, on the one side, a study of wealth and on the other, hand more important side, a part of study of man.'

Marshall, therefore, stressed the ultimate importance of man in the economic system. Marshall's definition is considered to be opposite welfare centered definition of Economics. The main features of Marshall's definition are:

1. **Study of material fundamentals of well-being:** These descriptions indicate that Economics discussed only the material aspects of well-being. Thus, these definitions emphasize the materialistic aspects of economic welfare.

2. **Concentrates on the ordinary business of life:** These definitions show that Economics associated with the study of man in the ordinary business of life. Thus, Economics discuss how an individual gets his income and how he uses it.

3. **A stress on the role of man:** These definitions stressed on the

role of man in creation of wealth or income.

**Alfred Marshall**

Alfred Marshall (26 July 1842 – 13 July 1924) was one of the most influential economists of his time and a founder of Economics. His book, *Principles of Economics* (1890), brought the ideas of supply and demand, marginal utility, and costs of production into a coherent whole.

## Criticism of Welfare Definition

Marshall's clarity of Economics works towards criticism. Robbins condemned Marshall's definition on several basis as follows:

## Wrong Concept of Material Goods:

Robbins mentioned that Marshall's definition includes within its purview only material things but it does not include non-material things which are things and non materials but are important. Such services are the services of the doctors, lawyers, teachers, etc, which are highly conducive to human welfare, and yet they have nothing material in them, although they are scarce and have value in them.

What is material and economic welfare?

Man earns money to get material welfare. Marshall's definition of Economics emphasized the study of wealth and humanity together, rather than wealth alone. Economic welfare broadly refers to the level of prosperity and living standards of either an individual or a group of persons. In the field of economics, it specifically refers to utility gained through the achievement of material goods and services. In other words, it refers to that part of social welfare that can be fulfilled through economic activity.

(i) Economics has no relation with the material welfare. According to Robbins, economics cannot be linked with material welfare mainly on account of (i) that concept of welfare cannot be defined precisely; (ii) we also study number of other activities which cannot be regarded as goods from the welfare point of view, for example, war, production of wine, opium, etc (iii) there is no appropriate scale of measurement through which welfare can be measured.

(ii) Wrong division of human activities: Division of human activities, according to Robbins, is also wrong because activities are neither completely economic nor non-economic, rather every activity has many aspects and one of them is economic aspect.

(i) Economics is a social science and it studies the economic activities of a social, normal and real man and not of beasts or animals or plants; (ii) Wealth is means while the end is human welfare; (iii) It studies the man's material welfare, not the whole of human welfare.

(iv) Material welfare cannot be quantitatively measured: Though money may be termed roughly measure, but certainly not a satisfactory measure of material welfare. We know that two persons paying the same price for a commodity do not derive same amount of the utility or satisfaction. The utility derived by the poor is much greater than utility that is derived by the rich person.

(v) Welfare definition is classificatory rather than analytical: Prof. Robbins mentioned that according to welfare definition economics concerns itself with certain group of activities rather than with the certain aspect of every activity. Thus according to Prof Robbins, human activity cannot be segregated and classified as economic, political, social and religious activities. Thus, an activity which though looks as non- economic initially but may turns out to be economic. For example, war is non economic activity but war gives rise to production of goods and budget of economy, hence it contains economic aspect.

**What is Neo-Classical Economics?**

Neoclassical economics is a term variously used for approaches to economics focusing on the determination of prices, outputs, and income distributions in markets through supply and demand, often mediated through a hypothesized maximization of utility by income-constrained individuals and of profits by cost-constrained firms employing available information and factors of production, in accordance with rational choice theory

From the above features of Marshall's definition, it is clear that Marshall said stress on material welfare as the primary apprehension of the science of economics. This definition explores the pasture of economic science to a larger study of humanity. Purposely, Marshall's vision is that economics studies all the events that people acquire in order to realize economic welfare. According to Marshall, "*man earns money to get material welfare*". This is why economists have termed his definition as the *welfare definition* of economics. This description puffed-up the scope of economic science by highlighting the study of wealth and humankind together, rather than wealth alone. Marshall is one of the economists who put in a high-quality work to economic theory. His explanation of economics engaged important place in economics from the disgrace it had fallen because of its connection with the study of wealth. He had sharpen out that wealth is not an end in itself but it is only a means to an end and the end being the endorsement of human welfare. Consequently, according to Marshall, wealth is only a minor things; man and his ordinary business of life, which is the key entity of economics study. In fact, Marshall tried to create the study of economics an train of social betterment.

## SCARCITY DEFINITION OF ECONOMICS

Prof. Lionel Robbins in his book '*Essays on the Nature and Significance of the Economic Science*', in print in 1932 enlarged a well defined and well-liked definition of Economics. Lionel Robbins, after

**Lionel Charles Robbins**
Charles Robbins, Baron Robbins, (22 November 1898 - 15 May 1984) was a British economist and head of the economics department at the London School of Economics.

criticizing the definition given by the Classical and Neo-classical economists, gave his own explanation of Economics. According to him, the definition of Economics given by him is better to that of others because it does not enclose any reference of the term material or welfare. **Secondly,** it narrates as much to the case of an remote individual as to the difficult net working of civilization. **Thirdly,** it lifts up the status of Economics to that of Science. **fourthly;** it makes Economics **'a positive science'** which deals only with facts. It prevents the economists to pass any value judgment of what is high-quality or bad, correct or incorrect, etc. According to him, human wants are unlimited, assets to satisfy them are limited and these resources have substitute uses.

> Economics is a science which studies human behavior as a relationship between ends and scare means which have alternative uses.- (p. 16)

Robbins's most famous book is *An Essay on the Nature and Significance of Economic Science*, contains three main thoughts. First is Robbins's famous all-inclusive definition of economics, tranquil used to define the subject today; second is the bold line Robbins drew between **positive and normative** issues. Positive matters are questions about what is; normative issues are about what have to to be. Robbins argued that economist should learn what is rather than what have to be. Robbins's third major thought is that **economics is a organization of logical deduction** from first principles. He was doubtful about the probability and convenience of empirical confirmation. A long line of economists after Robbins, including Scitovsky and Cassel agreed with this definition and carried on their analysis in line with this definition. It is a scarcity-based definition of Economics.

## What is logical deduction?

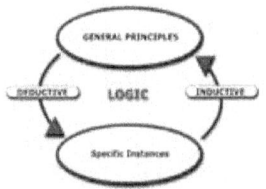

Deductive reasoning, also deductive logic or logical deduction or, informally, "top-down" logic, is the process of reasoning from one or more general statements (premises) to reach a logically certain conclusion. Deductive reasoning links premises with conclusions. An example of a deductive argument:

1. All men are mortal.
2. Aristotle is a man.
3. Therefore, Aristotle is mortal.

The first premise states that all objects classified as "men" have the attribute "mortal". The second premise states that "Aristotle" is classified as a "man" – a member of the set "men". The conclusion then states that "Aristotle" must be "mortal" because he inherits this attribute from his classification as a "man".

## Main Features of Scarcity Definition

The principal features of scarcity definitions are as follows:

**1. Human wants are unlimited:**

The scarcity definition of Economics states that human wants are unlimited. Human wants referred to as ends by Robbins are unlimited. They increase in quantity and quality over a period of time. They vary among individuals and overtime for the same individual. It is not possible to find a person who will say that his wants for goods and services have been completely satisfied. This is because of the fact that when one want is satisfied, it is replaced by another and there is then no end to it. The end of wants comes only with the end of life of a person.

## 2. Limited means to satisfy human wants:

Though wants are unlimited, yet the means for satisfying these wants are limited. The resources needed to satisfy these wants are limited. For example, the money income (per month) required for the satisfaction of wants of an individual is limited. Any resource is considered as scarce if its supply is less than its demand.

What is ends and means in Economics?

In economics the term 'ends' means the goals which a man wishes to achieve in the economic aspects of his life. The 'means' are the sources which are used to achieve the ends.

3. **Alternative uses of scarce resources:** Same resource can be devoted to alternative lines of production. Thus, same resource can be used for the satisfaction of different types of human wants. For example, a piece of land can be used for either cultivation, or building a dwelling place or building a factory shed, etc.

4. **Efficient use of scarce resources:** Since wants are unlimited, so these wants are to be ranked in order of priorities. On the basis of such priorities, the scarce resources are to be used in an efficient manner for the satisfaction of these wants. They are ranked in order

of significance as (a) necessaries (b) comforts and (c) luxuries. Man generally satisfies his urgent wants first and less urgent afterwards in order of their importance.

## 5. **Need for Choice and Optimization:**

Since human wants are unlimited, so one has to choose between the most urgent and less urgent wants. Hence, Economics is also called a science of choice. So, scarce resources are to be used for the maximum satisfaction (*i.e.,* optimization) of the most urgent human wants. Thus, there are many followers of Robbins explanation.

Robbins tries to make economics a more precise science. According to him, economics has not anything to do with ends. They may be dignified or dishonorable, material or non-material. Economics is not concerned with them by itself...an logical definition. Robbins definition makes the study of economics systematic. It studies the meticulous aspect of human behavior which is imposed by the power of scarcity.

**(iii)A worldwide definition:**

Robbins explanation is applicable everywhere. It is concerned with limitless wants and limited resources which is the problem facing every economy socialistic or capitalistic.

**(iv)Clear on the scenery and scope of economics:**

Robbins definition hands out to identify the nature, scope and subject matter of economics. According to him, an economic problem is distinguished by the likelihood of working out choice between ends and scarce means which have alternative uses.

**(v) Valuation is the central problem:**

According to Robbins, assessment is the central problem of economics. Wherever the ends are unlimited and the resources scarce, they give rise to an economic difficulty Marshall's definition does not identity this valuation process.

This definition is based on the following four pillars.

1.      Human needs or ends are unlimited.

2.      The ends diverge in significance.

3.      The means are limited.

4.      Means have substitute uses.

Scarcity is a reality of life. It happens among the poor and among the rich. The richest person on earth faces scarcity because he too cannot satisfy all his wants with the limited time available to him. According to Robbins, the limitless ends and the scarce resources offer a groundwork to the meadow of Economics. Since the human wants are innumerable and the means to satisfy them are restricted or inadequate in supply, thus, an economic problem happens. If all the things were abundantly available to satisfy the limitless human wants, there would not have arisen any shortage, hence no economic goods, no necessitate to economics and no economic problem. Scarcity, accordingly, can be defined as the overload of human wants over what can be really produced in the economy. The fourth, vital proposition of Robbins definition is that the scarce resources available to satisfy human wants have substitute uses. They can be placed to one use at one time. For example, if a piece of land is used for the production of rice, it cannot be utilized for the growth of

What are necessaries, comforts and luxuries goods?

Necessary goods are the basic requirement in day to day life without which we face problem in life existence such as basic food like rice, bread, lentils, shelter, clothing, etc. Comfort goods are which make life easier and happy such as TV, music system, fan, bicycle etc. On the other hand luxurious goods are those which are the symptoms courage, prestige, pride such as expensive car, jewelry etc. The definition of what necessities are has changed drastically over time, at any rate in western countries. A hundred years ago indoor plumbing for instance was regarded as a luxury, nowadays it is a necessity. Before World War One, a motor car was regarded as a luxury, only rich people had them. On the other hand, a hundred years ago servants were regarded as a necessity rather than a luxury. The better off you wee the more you would have. Nobody thought of doing without servants unless they were very poor.

another crop say vegetable at the same time. Man, therefore, has to decide the best way of utilizing the limited resources which have alternative uses. The lack of resources and unlimited choices are the key problems confronting every civilization.

Outline, the basis of economic science according to Robbins is based on fulfillment of human wants with limited resources which have alternative uses.

**Criticism on Robbins Definition**

Robbins definition has been resentfully disapproved by eminent writers like Hicks, Durbin, Frazer, etc., on the subsequent reasons:

**1) Compact economics just to a theory of value:**

Robbin's definition limits the span of economics by treating it as a positive science only at the same time as in reality it is both a positive and a normative science

**(2). Scope of economics has been widened:**

Robbin's definition has widened the scope of economics by casing the whole of economic time, while it is concerned with that part of human life which is associated with the marketplace price.

**(3) Economics has become a neutral science:**

Robbin's definition has made economics neutral, unfriendly and nonfigurative. It is in fact a description of economics for economist only.

**(5)  Study of economic growth:**

The study of economic growth process remains exterior the range of economics while it is from side to side economic growth that livelihood principles improve.

Thus, the definition of economics given by Robbins has no doubt convinced failings. However, it is more all-inclusive in unfolding the difficulty of resource utilization.

# 3. BASIC ECONOMIC DILEMMA OF SOCIETY

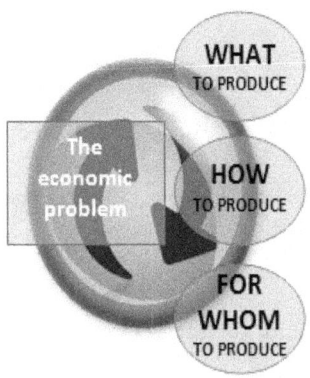

The capacity of economics entails the identification of basic economic problems before any society and find out different possible ways to solve those problems.

1. What goods shall be produced and in what amount?

2. How should the various goods and services be produced?

3. How should the goods and services be distributed?

## (i) What to Produce?

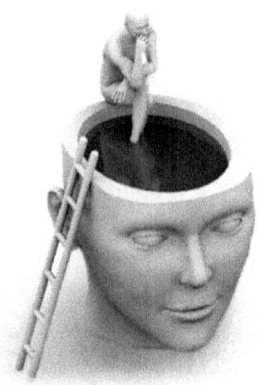

The very first question that any economic system must answer is: What goods and services are to be produced in a society and in what quantities? This question arises from the fact that human wants are *unlimited,* while resources are *limited.* The satisfaction of human wants requires the consumption of goods and services. Human beings, therefore, wish to consume goods and services. But, since resources are limited, the economic system cannot produce *all* types of goods and services. Even any particular good or service cannot be produced in an infinitely large quantity. Only *finite* amounts of a *limited number* of goods and services can be produced. Therefore, there arises this decision problem. The economy must decide which goods and services to produce and which goods and services to exclude from production. The economy must *choose* its production plan carefully. Everything cannot be produced and even those things which are produced cannot be produced in unlimited quantities.

## How to Produce?

The second basic problem that every economy must solve is that of deciding *how to produce* the goods and services (that the economy has decided to produce). A particular quantity of a particular good or service can be produced in many different ways. The economy must choose a particular way of producing the specified amount of the good. Moreover, this must be done for each of the different goods and services that the economy wants to produce.

In the language of the economists, a particular way of producing a particular good or service (or a set of goods and services) is called a *technique of production*. For instance, in some cases, a particular amount of a particular good can be produced by different combinations of inputs. Thus, it may be that 10 tons of wheat can be produced either on 2 hectares of land by 5 agricultural workers or on 4 hectares of land by 2 workers. Here, there are two techniques for producing 10 tons of wheat: (2 hectares of land, 5 workers) and (4 hectares of land,

2 workers). An economy which has decided to produce 10 tons of wheat must choose between these two techniques. There is a similar problem for every good (or every set of goods). Therefore, the question 'how to produce' is also known as the problem of *choice of techniques.*

## Whom to Produce?

Suppose now that the first two basic problems have been solved *i.e.,* the economy has decided the amounts of production of various goods and services and has also chosen the appropriate techniques for producing them. There still remains the problem of deciding the manner in which the produced goods and services will be used. That will, obviously, be used to satisfy human wants. But among the members of society, who will receive how much of the produced commodities? In other words, after the commodities have been *produced,* there remains the task of deciding how they will be *distributed.*

Who will get (to consume) the produced commodities? This is known as the question: '*for whom to produce?* It is also known as the *problem of distribution.*

## GROWTH-ORIENTED DEFINITION:

Robbins's scarcity description was no hesitation more broad scientific and acceptable and that is why it was extensively used in economic literature. But lately, the contemporary economist like J. M. Keynes, Benham, and Samuelson have considered Robbins's scarcity definition unacceptable for the current growth oriented world. So they have given a contemporary description of Economics. In moderately modern times, more broad definitions of Economics have been offered. A large number of modern economists devoted to this broad definition of Economics.

## Paul A. Samuelson

Paul Anthony Samuelson (May 15, 1915 – December 13, 2009) was an American economist, and the first American to win the Nobel Memorial Prize in Economic Sciences. Samuelson had been awarded prestigious Nobel Prize for the year 1970 for the scientific work through which he has developed static and dynamic economic theory and actively contributed to raising the level of analysis in economic science. *The New York Times* considered him to be the "foremost academic economist of the 20th century".

According to Paul A. Samuelson "Economics is the study of how men and society choose with or without the use of money to employ scarce productive resources which could have alternative uses to produce various commodities over time and distribute them for consumption now and in the future amongst various people and groups of society".

According to J.M. Keynes, "Economics studies how the levels of national income and employment in the community are determined and how the national income grows over years".

According to the description of the modern economists, Economics is not only a discuss the allocation of scarce resources but also a discuss of how the means can be further enlarged to protect maximum happiness of wants and how the levels of income and employ in a county are determined and how national income develops over years. Features of the Modern Growth-Oriented Definition are:

## 1. Growth-Orientation:

Economic growth is measured by the change in national output over time. The definition says that, Economics is concerned with determining the pattern of employment of scarce resources to produce commodities 'over time'. Thus, the dynamic problems of manufacture have been brought within the purview of Economics.

### J.M. Keynes

John Maynard Keynes, 1st Baron Keynes, (5 June 1883 – 21 April 1946) was a British economist whose ideas have affected the theory and practice of modern macroeconomics, and informed the economic policies of Govts. He built on and greatly refined earlier work on the causes of business cycles, and is widely considered to be one of the founders of modern macroeconomics and the most influential economist of the 20th century. His ideas are the basis for the school of thought known as Keynesian economics, as well as its various offshoots. His most revolutionary book was 'The general theory of interest and money.

## 2. Active allocation of consumption:

Similarly, under this definition, Economics is relates with the pattern of consumption, not only now but also in the future. Thus, the problem of dividing the use of income between present consumption and future consumption has been brought within the orbit of Economics.

## 3. Distribution:

The modern description also distresses itself with the distribution of consumption among various persons and groups in a society. Thus, while the problem of distribution is implicit in the earlier definitions, the modern definition makes it explicit.

## 1. Improvement of resource allocation:

The definition also says that, Economics analyses the costs and benefits of improving the pattern of resource allocation. Improvement of resource allocation and better distributive justice are synonymous with economic development. Thus, issues of development of a less developed economy have also been made subjects of the study of Economics.

To put it summarily, the modern definition of Economics is the most comprehensive of all the definitions. All the issues that were highlighted in the earlier definitions are included here. In addition, the issues of development of a backward economy, as well as those of growth in a mature capitalist economy, form part of this definition. Economics as it stands today is built on the basis of this comprehensive definition.

### What is Economic growth?

Economic growth is the increase in the amount of the goods and services produced by an economy over time. It is conventionally measured as the percent rate of increase in *real gross domestic product*, or *real GDP*.

**Robbins Definition:**

Prof. Samuelson has also stressed the problem of scarcity of means in relation to limited ends, dynamical part of definition similar to Robbins definition. The phases used in Samuelson definition, such as 'to produce various commodities over time' and distribute them for consumption now and in future were intended to stress the dynamic nature of the definition. Therefore, the Samuelson definition is built up on the basis provided by Robbins' definition. All elements in Robbins definition are inherent in Samuelson definition also. Dynamic content of Sam nelson's definition is wider than Robbins definition: Because it is applicable even in barter economy. A barter economy too is confronted with the scarcity of means in relation to ends. Samuelson's definition deals the problem of choice in its dynamic setting: The problem of choice relates not only to present, but also to the future. We know that human wants never remain fixed or static. They continually change with the lapse of time and also become multiple. The multiplication of wants also gives rise to the necessity of bringing about corresponding changes in resources. Therefore, the Samuelson definition is built up on the basis provided by Robbins' definition. All elements in Robbins definition are inherent in Samuelson definition also. Dynamic content of Sam nelson's definition is wider than Robbins definition: Because it is applicable even in barter economy. A barter economy too is confronted with the scarcity of means in relation to ends. Samuelson's definition deals the problem of choice in its dynamic setting: The problem of choice relates not only to present, but also to the future. We know that human wants never remain fixed or static. They continually change with the lapse of time and also become multiple. The multiplication of wants also gives rise to the necessity of bringing about corresponding changes in resources.

After considering the various definitions of Economics, we can easily conclude that none of them is satisfactory. If we exclude man and his welfare from the study of Economics, there will be no use of studying it: If we define Economics as a science of administration of scare resources, then its scope becomes too wide and includes the whole of economics life and not merely that part of it which is connected with the market price. Economics is the science which studies the activities related to the most efficient consumption, production, exchange and distribution of the scarce means, having alternative uses, for the maximum satisfaction of the human wants, for increasing welfare and for economic development.

# 4 SCOPE OF ECONOMICS

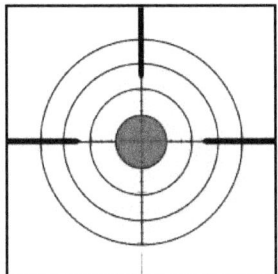

The scope of economics is the area or boundary of the study of economics. In scope of economics we answer and analyze the following three main questions.

(1) What is the subject matter of economics?

(2) What is the nature of economics?

(3) What are the limitations of economics?

## 1. Subject matter of Economics.

There is a difference of opinion among economists regarding the subject-matter of Economics. Adam. Smith, the father of modern Economic Theory, defined Economics as a subject, which is mainly concerned with the study of nature and causes of generation of wealth of nation. Impressed by the condemnation of the 19th century writers, like Carlyle and Ruskin, Marshall introduced the concept of welfare in the study of Economics. According to Marshall "Economics is a study of mankind in the ordinary business of life. It examines that part of individual and social actions which is closely connected with the material requisites of well being". In this definition, Marshall has shifted the emphasis from wealth to man. He gives primary importance to man and secondary importance to wealth.

The Robin's concept of the subject-matter of Economics is that "Economics is a science which studies human behaviour as a relationship between ends and scarce means which have alternative uses". According to Robbins (i) human wants are unlimited (ii) means at his disposal to satisfy these wants are not only limited, (iii) but have alternative uses. Man is always busy in adjusting his limited resources for the satisfaction of unlimited ends. The problems that centre "round such activities constitute the subject-matters of Economics.

What is science and art?

**Science:** The word Science derived from Latin word *scientia*, which means knowledge is a systematic enterprise that builds and organizes knowledge in the form of testable explanations and predictions about the universe. According to Aristotle, "science" refers to the body of reliable knowledge itself, of the type that can be logically and rationally explained.

**Art:** Art is a diverse range of human activities and the products of those activities; this article focuses primarily on the visual arts, which includes the creation of images or objects in fields including painting, sculpture, printmaking, photography, and other visual media.

Paul A Samuelson, however, includes the dynamic aspects of economics in the subject matter. According to him, Economics is the study of how man and society choose with or without money, to employ productive uses to produce various commodities over time and distribute them for consumption now and in future among various people and groups of society".

# 5 NATURE OF ECONOMICS

The economists are also divided regarding the nature of economics. The following questions are generally covered in the nature of economics

(i)     Is economics a science or arts?

(ii)    Is it a positive science or a normative science?

(1) Economics as a science or an art. Economics is both a science and an art. Economics is considered as a science because it is a systematic knowledge derived from observation, study and experimentation. However, the degree of perfection of economics laws is less compared with the laws of pure sciences.

An art is the practical application of knowledge for achieving definite ends. A science teaches us to know a phenomenon and an art teaches us to do a thing. For example, there is inflation in Pakistan. This information is derived from positive science. The government takes certain fiscal and monetary measures to bring down the general level of prices in the country. The study of these fiscal and monetary measures to bring down inflation makes the subject of economics as an art.

After arriving at a conclusion that economics is both a science as well as an art, here arises another controversy. Is economics a positive science or a normative science?

Economics as a positive or normative science. There is again difference of opinions among economists whether economics is a positive or normative science. Lionel Robbins, Senior and Friedman have described economics as a positive science. They opined that economics is based on logic. It is a value theory only. It is, therefore, neutral between ends.

## What is positive and normative science?

Positive science implies that science which establishes relationship between cause and effect. In other words, it scientifically analyses a problem and examines the causes of a problem.

For example, if prices have gone up, why have they gone up? In short, problems are examined on the basis of facts. On the other hand, normative science relates to normative aspects of a problem *i.e.,* what ought to be. Under normative science, conclusions and results are not based on facts, rather they are based on different considerations like social, cultural, political, religious and son are basically is subjective in nature, an expression of opinions. In short, positive science is concerned with 'how and why' and normative science with 'what ought to be'. The distinction between the two can be explained with the help of an example of increase in the rate of interest. Under positive science it would be looked into as to why interest rate has gone up and how can it be reduced whereas under normative science it would be seen as to whether this increase is good or bad. Three statements about positive and normative science each are given below:

Marshall, Pigou, Hawtrey, Keynes and many other economists

regard economics as a normative science. According to them, the real function of the Science is, to increase the well-being of man. They have given suggestions in their works for promotion of human welfare. For example, Malthus has given suggestions of checking the rising population. J.M. Keynes has 'suggested measures to remove unemployment.

## TECHNIQUE OF ECONOMIC ANALYSIS

Economic theory are the derive laws or generalizations through two methods (1) Deductive Method and (2) Inductive Method. These two ways of deriving economic simplification are now explain in concise form below.

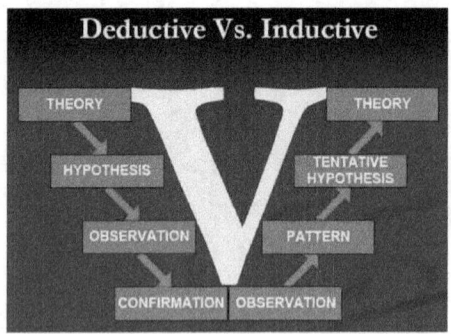

## 1. Deductive Method.

The deductive method is also named as logical, theoretical or preceding method. The deductive method consists in deriving conclusions from universal truths. It acquires a few general principles and applies them to draw conclusions. For instance, if we accept the general proposition that man is entirely provoked by self-interest; Ram is a man; therefore, the inference will be drawn that Ram is provoked by self-interest. In applying the deductive method of economic investigation, we proceed from universal to scrupulous. The classical and neo-classical school of economists particularly, Ricardo. Mill, Cairnes, Marshall, Malthus Pigou etc. have applied the deductive method in their economic analysis. The main steps involved in deductive logic are as under:

### (1) Insight of the problem to be inquires into:

In the process of deriving simplification, the analyst must have a obvious and exact idea of the problem to be inquired into.

**(2)    The terms:**

The next step is to define evidently the scientific terms to be used in economic analysis. Further, the suppositions made for a theory should also be exact.

**(3)    Presuming hypothesis from the assumptions:**

The third step in deriving simplifications is deducing hypothesis from the presumptions taken.

**(4)    Hypothesis Testing**

Prior to the establishment of law or generalization, the hypothesis should be confirmed through direct observations of actions in the real humankind and through statistical techniques (There is a direct relationship between price and quantity supplied of a good is a well established generalization).

## Advantages of Deductive Method:

The main qualities of deductive method are as under:

(1) This method is near to realism. It is not as much of time taking and less exclusive.

(2) The utilization of mathematical techniques in deducing laws of economics conveys accuracy and simplicity in economic analysis.

(3) There being limited scope of testing in economics, the method helps in gaining economic theories.

(4) The method is straightforward because it is logical.

## Disadvantages of Deductive method

It is true that deductive method is easy and accurate, if the underlying presumptions are valid. There is 'IF', in the statement. The inadequacies of the deductive approach are as under:

(1) The deductive method is simple and accurate only if the underlying assumptions are valid. More often the presumptions

produce to be based on half truth or have no relation to realism. The results drawn from such presumptions will, therefore, be ambiguous.

(2) Prof. Learner explains the deductive technique as *"Armchair"* analysis. According to him, the grounds from which deductions are drawn may not hold good at all periods, and places. As such deductive reasoning's are not appropriate generally.

(3) The deductive method is highly hypothetical. It needs a great deal of worry to keep away from dreadful, basis or defective economic analysis. As the deductive method employed by the classical and neo-classical economists led to many simplistic results due to dependence on imperfect and wrong presumptions, therefore, under the German Historical School of economists, a pointed reaction began against this method. They promote a more practical method for economic analysis known as inductive method.

**Inductive Method**

Inductive method which is also termed empirical method was accepted by the historical **"School of economists**. It engaged the process of analysis from particular details to general standard. This method acquires economic generalization the basis of (1) Experimentations (2) Observations and (3) Statistical Techniques. The main steps involved in the application of inductive method are: (i) observation (ii) formation of hypothesis (iii) generalization and (iv) verification

## Advantages of Inductive Method

(1)   It is based on particulars as such the method is sensible.

(2)   In order to examine the economic values, the method makes use of statistical techniques. The inductive method is, thus, more dependable.

(3)   Inductive method is active. The altering economic phenomenon are analyzed and on the basis of data, conclusion and results are drawn from them.

(4)   Induction method also helps in expectations of investigations.

## Disadvantages of inductive method:

The main flaws of this method are as under:

(1) If conclusions are drawn from inadequate data, the generalizations obtained prettiness.

(2) The collection of data itself is not a simple job. The basis and techniques employed in the collection of data differ from researcher to investigator. The outcomes, therefore, may vary even with the same dilemma.

**(3) The inductive method is time overwhelming and exclusive.**

The above analysis reveals that both the methods have drawbacks. We cannot rely solely on any one of methods. Modern economists are of the view that both these methods are flattering. They are associates and not opponent. 'Alfred Marshall has truly comments, 'Inductive and Deductive methods are both needed for scientific thought, the right and left foot is both needed for walking". We can relate any of them or both as the condition demands.

******

www.ingramcontent.com/pod-product-compliance
Lightning Source LLC
Chambersburg PA
CBHW070934180526
45168CB00003B/1072